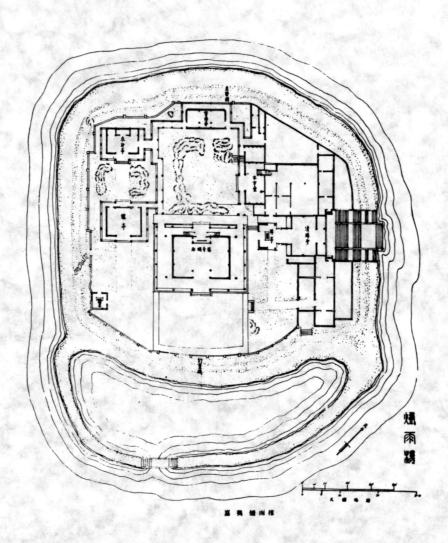

There are visual similarities between
the plan of the Chinese garden above,
and the Chinese character of 'garden'
on the opposite page.

壬戌夏苦步園多嵩覚恆

The Art Of Chinese Gardens

THE ART OF CHINESE GARDENS

Chung Wah Nan, RIBA

HONG KONG UNIVERSITY PRESS 1982

ISBN 962-209-059-1

Printed and bound in Hong Kong
by Hip Shing Offset Printing Factory,
and Ching Yick Printing & Book Binding Co. Ltd.

To My Parents

The Art of Chinese Gardens

It is often forgotten that the gardens we see in China today were once parts of the private residences of high officials, mandarins and wealthy merchants.

Confiscated by the governments of various emperors from the sixteenth right up to the twentieth century they were often used as government offices and sometimes even as dormitories for soldiers. However, the gardens have seen glorious days filled with laughter and song, used for opera and sumptuous banquets and peopled, as honourable guests, artists, poets, calligraphers and men-of-letters thus gratifying the serenity, meditation, quietness of spirit and soul that these Elysian vistas engendered.

The gardens have witnessed their own dilapidation of crumbling walls and rotting rafters; have been dwelt in by rats and snakes and other destructive pests. Some have not escaped total destruction at the hands of man and nature. Fortunately, some gardens have miraculously survived the ravages of time, fate and the Cultural Revolution. Many private gardens and temples have been reduced to ruins through the rampages of the 'Sixties'. It is therefore a wonder that some gardens remain for us to view – perhaps not as the original owners viewed them – but many are partly, if not completely, restored. At least they look authentic.

An amazing phenomenon is that the younger generation now love to throng those gardens which at one time they had helped to destroy. Young people are again – as did their ancestors – appreciating the mystery and joy of tortuous rocks and illogically twisted footpaths that help to infuse a sense of peace and quietism. As with young leaves in spring, young people sprout out of the old bare trunk that is China, continuing the rejuvenation that is the continuation of life itself.

It is our good fortune that gardens have been and are being restored to their former splendour with tremendous effort. They are being opened to the public in China (and to foreign visitors) resulting in a significant revival of interest in both their use – as the originators envisaged – and their natural beauty. As with Beijing (Peking) opera, Chinese gardens are surviving all previous turmoils and like the young leaves rejuvenating the traditions of this long neglected culture.

The art of Chinese gardens dates back to the fifth century and was cultivated throughout the succeeding dynasties, achieving its pinnacle in the sixteenth century. It is therefore not possible to show the development either historically or chronologically by photographs in a small book. I can only resort to my professional tools with which I propose to analyse this ancient art architecturally. An attempt which may be inadequate but at least which represents a personal approach to the understanding of man's desire to be in harmony with the vast universe through physical means.

This attempt is particularly meaningful when the world's populations are concentrating in industrial and commercial cities; when urban living is forcing us to divorce ourselves from nature; when our children grow up among electronic toys and factory-produced food; when the majority of us stay in pigeon-hole dwellings that are mass produced in concrete; when even natural materials can be simulated in plastic forms and we forget what genuine wood, stone, or lawn grass look like; when competition for survival is so keen that we accept stress as a way of life and fail to appreciate the murmur of a running stream, the budding of flowers, and the rugged beauty of a piece of rock.

I invite my fellow sufferers to stop and pause for a moment; to look at these pictures to enjoy both nature itself and man's attempts to enhance it. If for a fleeting moment, you share the joy of Chinese gardens – the folding skin of rocks, the shadow of bamboo dancing on a white wall, the silhouette of dark eaves against the bright sky, the smooth flat surface of water turning to ripples, the sound of a wind bell, all the simple joy of nature – then I am content.

Perhaps in this synthetic world of ours the meaning of the Chinese gardens will one day bring us to terms with nature, especially in the appreciation of raw materials. Perhaps in this time of utilitarianism a little 'esoteric' knowledge can be a good antidote to our computerized life.

'Curious learning not only makes unpleasant things less unpleasant, but also makes pleasant things more pleasant.'

Encouraged by this remark of Bertrand Russell, I share my study of Chinese gardens with you.

Chung Wah Nan
April 1982

始

In the Beginning

'In the beginning there were air mists; and spouts came forth from the soil; and heaven and earth were divided; and then came the sun and the moon; and the *yin* and the *yang* were differentiated and united to form a neutral womb which gave birth to Pan Ku. Pan Ku was the first man, a giant of a man.'*

When he died his body became mountains, his hair turned into forest and his blood flew into rivers. Pan Ku was beautiful in all his rugged splendour. Through his folding skin I perceive strength and tenderness; I still see his flesh in soil and bones in rocks. I feel his growing (or shall I say germinating) silently at night; sometimes he sighs that we have misshaped him. At other times he gets angry and throws himself into a rage and calls in rain and thunder and the earth trembles.

*盤古氏, author's translation.

Shi Lin
(Stone Forest)
YUNNAN

雲南　石林
1980 年

Shi Lin
(Stone Forest)
YUNNAN

雲南　石林
1980 年

Shi Lin
(Stone Forest)
YUNNAN

雲南　石林
1980 年

Shi Lin
(Stone Forest)
YUNNAN

雲南　石林
1980 年

11

Chang Jiang
(Yangtze River)
SICHUAN

四川　長江三峽
　　1980 年

15

Chang Jiang
(Yangtze River)
SICHUAN

四川　長江
　1980 年

Chang Jiang
(Yangtze River)
SICHUAN

四川　長江
1980 年

天成

Man-made or Natural?

When Pan Ku is tender, young leaves spring forth and birds sing; when he is shy he is withdrawn, shrouded in mist and fog and deep mystery. I walk into him and discover caves, shelters, gateways and ponds. I peek and I seek and find him at last – you Pan Ku, my dear Great Earth – a garden in disguise!

From seeming chaos I perceive order; from death I perceive rebirth. You have not died! You have given hints to us of a garden made out of you.

Shi Lin
(Stone Forest)
YUNNAN

雲南　石林
　1980 年

23

Shi Lin
(Stone Forest)
YUNNAN

雲南　石林
1980 年

雲南　石林
1980 年

Dong Hu
(East Lake)
SHAOXING

紹興 東湖
1979 年

29

蘇州　虎丘
1979 年

杭州 靈隱寺
1979 年

Hu Qiu
(Tiger Hill)
SUZHOU

蘇州　虎丘
1979 年

廣州　街景
1979 年

Creation of Space

'By studying the organic patterns of heaven and earth a fool can become a sage; and so by watching the times and seasons of natural phenomena we can become true philosophers.'

An eighth century Tang poet summed up human curiosity towards the universe. The Chinese garden is therefore a miniature universe in which one observes and lives with the time and seasons, and for centuries ways and means have been devised to achieve this aim.

The simplest way is to frame up the objects one wishes to observe as one does with a painting.

This group of pictures shows the 'framing' technique from the initially two-dimensional ways to the increasingly complicated three-dimensional methods. Note how space and distance are created.

蘇州　留園
1979 年

杭州　玉泉
1979 年

Liu Yuan
(Liu Garden)
SUZHOU

蘇州　留園
1979 年

入勝

蘇州　獅子林
1979 年

Shizi Lin
(Lion Forest)
SUZHOU

蘇州　獅子林
1979 年

蘇州　虎丘

蘇州 怡園
1979 年

Hu Qiu
(Tiger Hill)
SUZHOU

蘇州　虎丘
1979年

55

Yin-Yang

'In order to remain intact, be dented.
In order to keep straight, be bent.
In order to be filled, be hollowed. Less is more.'*

These seemingly contradictory remarks by Lao Tze were made some time in 500 BC.

The *yin-yang* principle is not contradictory at all as it is nature itself.
'In order to see the bright day one must live through the dark night.'

In Chinese calligraphy the basic principle of brush technique is:
'In order to go right you must go left first; in order to go down you must go up first.'

In terms of design the *yin-yang* principle can be simply interpreted as the rule of contrasts.

Photographs in this section demonstrate the most important technique in Chinese garden design. You will see dark interiors against the bright outside world, white walls, dark eaves and roofs against the bright sky, hard irregular rocks against the soft smooth water, curved edges against straight lines.

I like to use the last picture of this group to summarize this mystery. When two forces act in opposite directions, there lies the secret of all creation.

Tao Te Ching, author's translation.

Lingyan Si
(Lingyan Temple)
SUZHOU

蘇州　靈岩寺
1979 年

59

Canglang Ting
(Canglang Pavilion)
SUZHOU

蘇州　滄浪亭
1979 年

杭州　六和塔
1979 年

Yu Yuan
(Yu Garden)
SHANGHAI

上海　豫園
1979 年

無錫　寄暢園
1979 年

Liu Yuan
(Liu Garden)
SUZHOU

蘇州 留園
1979 年

Liu Yuan
(Liu Garden)
SUZHOU

蘇州　留園
1979 年

Zhuozheng Yuan
(Zhuozheng Garden)
SUZHOU

蘇州　拙政園
1979 年

Yi Yuan
(Yi Garden)
SUZHOU

蘇州　怡園
1979 年

Buildings

Buildings in the Chinese garden are necessary but of secondary importance. The garden occupies the best part of the lot. A quick reference to the plans will show that buildings are normally grouped tightly on the periphery of the land and near the street. The Western approach would be just the opposite. The Chinese garden is the sanctuary for the inhabitants. Inside the house one does not mind some noise from the street. When one is walking inside the garden or sitting idle in a pavilion one must not be disturbed by the outside world but surrounded by trees, rocks and water or birds.

Buildings are inevitably planned symmetrically. Gardens are always planned irregularly or organically.

Buildings are hidden by trees, rocks and walls. Sometimes buildings can be easily seen but not easily accessible, due to a twisting footpath or a crooked bridge.

Shizi Lin
(Lion Forest)
SUZHOU

蘇州　獅子林
1979 年

Shizi Lin
(Lion Forest)
SUZHOU

蘇州 獅子林
1979 年

Dushu Tai
(Reading Terrace)
CHANGSHU

常熟 讀書台
1979 年

Liu Yuan
(Liu Garden)
SUZHOU

蘇州　留園
1979 年

蘇州 拙政園
1979 年

Liu Yuan
(Liu Garden)
SUZHOU

蘇州　留園
1979 年

Hu Qiu
(Tiger Hill)
SUZHOU

蘇州　虎丘
1979 年

。 **昆明** 民居
1980 年

Water

Water is one of the Five Elements, others being Metal, Wood, Fire and Earth. A garden without the element of water is a blind garden.

Water takes the shape of its container. A regular shaped pool is mechanical and strangles the water it contains.

Water: the generator of life
        the mirage of reality
        the eye of the garden.

杭州　西湖
1979 年

昆明　民居
1979 年

Village
WUXI

無錫　民居
1979年

Dong Hu
(East Lake)
SHAOXING

Xi Hu
(West Lake)
HANGZHOU

杭州　西湖
1979 年

Xi Hu
(West Lake)
HANGZHOU

杭州　西湖
1979 年

107

Zhuozheng Yuan
(Zhuozheng Garden)
SUZHOU

蘇州　拙政園
1979 年

Zhuozheng Yuan
(Zhuozheng Garden)
SUZHOU

蘇州　拙政園
1979 年

拙政園
979 年

Xi Hu
(West Lake)
HANGZHOU

杭州　西湖
1979 年

115

隔

Walls, Footpaths and Paving

Walls have been extensively used in China to provide defence, protection and privacy. There are the Great Wall, city walls, palace walls and the residential garden walls and courtyard walls.

In gardens the walls are used to define space and create distance or depth.

They are used as white back drops for displaying rocks and trees.

Objects hidden behind a wall create mystery.

Walls are used to screen, direct and control visual as well as physical explorations.

They work in conjunction with footpaths.

Together they help visitors to play the game of hide-and-seek.

To hide is to increase the fun of seeking.

Liu Yuan
(Liu Garden)
SUZHOU

蘇州 留園
1979 年

蘇州　靈岩寺
1979 年

Liu Yuan
(Liu Garden)
SUZHOU

蘇州　留園
1979 年

123

蘇州　留園

上海　豫園

1979 年

無錫　寄暢園
1979 年

Hu Qiu
(Tiger Hill)
SUZHOU

蘇州　虎丘
1979 年

131

無錫 蠡園
1979 年

Gu Shan
(Lonely Hill)
HANGZHOU

州 孤山
1979 年

蘇州　留園

蘇州　留園

Windows and Doors

'We shape clay into an urn. It is the empty void that makes it useful.
We form doors and windows for a house. It is through these empty
voids that the house becomes useful.'*

Who else but Lao Tze could have thought of such a wonderful description.

I sincerely believe that some walls are deliberately erected so that doors and windows
can be created.

*Tao Te Ching, author's translation.

Liu Yuan
(Liu Garden)
SUZHOU

蘇州　留園
1979 年

Yule Yuan
(Yule Garden)
HANGZHOU

杭州　魚樂園
1979 年

蘇州　留園
1979 年

杭州　魚樂園
1979 年

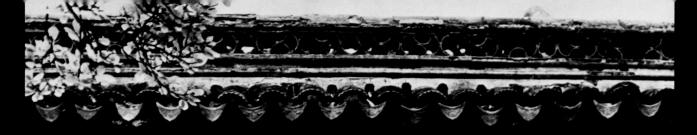

Shizi Lin
(Lion Forest)
SUZHOU

蘇州　獅子林
1979 年

153

Wangshi Yuan
(Wangshi Garden)
SUZHOU

蘇州　網師園
1979 年

155

紹興　廟園
1979 年

Temple courtyard
SHAOXING

紹興　廟園
1979 年

Wangshi Yuan
(Wangshi Garden)
SUZHOU

蘇州　網師園
1979 年

161

蘇州　獅子林
1979 年

Wangshi Yuan
(Wangshi Garden)
SUZHOU

蘇州　網師園
1979 年

Town residence
SUZHOU

蘇州　民居
1979 年

Bridges

In Chinese Buddhist terminology 'arriving at the shore opposite' means one has lived through one's useful life. In order to arrive at the opposite shore one of the simplest ways is to walk across a bridge.

Living through one's life is like crossing over a bridge.

The streams or ponds are therefore prepared so that beautiful bridges can be created!

Architecturally a bridge is an interlink between two different spaces.

Psychologically a bridge is an intermission through which one prepares onself for a new space.

This group of photographs shows various types of bridges including a minute one used by ants.

蘇州　留園
1979 年

廣州　蘭甫
1980 年

Dong Hu
(East Lake)
SHAOXING

紹興　東湖
1979 年

175

Xi Hu
(West Lake)
HANGZHOU

杭州　西湖
1979 年

177

蘇州　拙政園
1979 年

杭州　西湖
1979 年

蘇州　虎丘
1979 年

經
緯

Vertical Element

Verticality is inherent in nature in the forms of trees, rocks and mountains.

It breaks the monotony of horizontality.

A stele with carved Buddhist scripture makes the visitor look up to it with reverence and respect. The free form of a tall boulder is for joy and verticality. The towering pagoda is a vertical architectural expression. Originally pagodas were built for storing Buddhist scripture. Later on they were built as viewpoints, like an observation tower which is 'borrowed' by nearby gardens so that the hill with the pagoda can be viewed within the various gardens as part of the gardens themselves.

上海郊　古猗園
1979 年

蘇州　怡園
1979 年

Liu Yuan
(Liu Garden)
SUZHOU

蘇州　留園
1979 年

191

Shizi Lin
(Lion Forest)
SUZHOU

蘇州　獅子林
1979 年

193

蘇州　留園
1979 年

Canglang Ting
(Canglang Pavilion)
SUZHOU

蘇州　滄浪亭
1979 年

杭州　靈隱寺
1979 年

Lingyan Si Ta
(Lingyan Temple Pagoda)
SUZHOU

蘇州　靈岩寺塔
1979 年

201

Beisi Ta
(Beisi Pagoda)
SUZHOU

蘇州　北寺塔
1979 年

203

無錫　寄暢園
1979 年

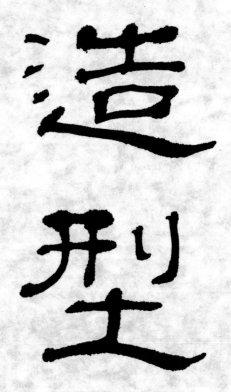

Sculpture

Sculptures in the Chinese garden are modest compared with their counterparts for religious and burial purposes. Yet there is a primitive quality to them which is more earthy and genuine. The folklore element assumes a decorative role without being overpowering. Larger scale pieces are used in temples and palatial gardens.

Sculpture in gardens is freer and more imaginative. The huge 'Island floating on the Sea' piece in the Summer Palace garden has a well-carved sea with stylized waves on an oval base, which has a rugged and uncarved natural rock top. The contrast is very pleasing.

The grotesque Taiwu lake rocks can be arranged to imitate flying birds or lions and to the untrained eye they are just abstract sculpture. Boulders can be arranged with trees to form a small composition here and there. These miniature compositions are hidden everywhere for the visitor to seek out.

Zhuozheng Yuan
(Zhuozheng Garden)
SUZHOU

蘇州　拙政園
1979 年

209

Temple
KUNMING

昆明　廟宇
1980 年

Xi Hu
(West Lake)
HANGZHOU

杭州　西湖
1979 年

213

昆明　圓通寺
1980 年

廣州　蘭甫
1980年

Shizi Lin
(Lion Forest)
SUZHOU

蘇州　獅子林
1979 年

219

北京　頤和園
1979 年

Lan Pu
(Orchid Nursery)
GUANGZHOU

廣州　蘭甫
1980 年

Lan Pu
(Orchid Nursery)
GUANGZHOU

廣州　蘭甫
1980 年

Hu Qiu
(Tiger Hill)
SUZHOU

蘇州　虎丘
1979 年

蘇州　網師園

書
法

Calligraphy

Chinese calligraphy is the one art that integrates with the daily life of the ordinary people as well as the more educated élite. From the oracle bones to the present day new year red couplets, calligraphy is appreciated and treasured by all.

In the Chinese garden calligraphy is carved on stone, wood and rock.

Carved stone slabs are embedded in corridors. These are collector's pieces by famous calligraphers. Those on top of entrances are normally the name of the hall or garden, denoting the nature of the place you are about to enter.

The couplets express the calligrapher's wishes in life, or describe the scene or the building. This unique association between art and building or garden can only be found in Chinese culture.

Yu Yuan
(Yu Garden)
SHANGHAI

上海　豫園
1974 年

233

蘇州　網師園
1979 年

文章華國
詩禮傳家
岳飛題

五代攟枭克汗頭
三聲弓除開氏血

岳飛

Hanshan Si
(Hanshan Temple)
SUZHOU

蘇州 寒山寺
1979 年

239

Yuantong Si
(Yuantong Temp
KUNMING

明　圓通寺
1980 年

Jin Dian
(Golden Templ
KUNMING

福

帝道满三千上菩醯飛無雙玉宇無雙地

天合高百尺東林竹舞一半寿山一半雲

昆明　金殿
1980年

Yu Yuan
(Yu Garden)
SHANGHAI

上海　豫園
1974 年

24

蘇州　獅子林
1979 年

蘇州　滄浪亭
1979 年

Liu Yuan
(Liu Garden)
SUZHOU

蘇州 留園
1979 年

簡介

中國園林是一種綜合性的藝術，它是由園藝、建築、繪畫、雕塑、詩詞、書法相承互構而成的一種綜合藝術；而這種綜合藝術是中國獨有的。如果把風鈴、流水、秋聲也當作刻意經營的音調，那麼，中國園林可稱爲世界上最早、最全面的環境設計了。

要把文人對人造環境的詩意營造出來，是要靠豐富而又有長久歷史的工匠。試問如果沒有這兩者之間的默契和意會，又怎能把「望之如在野，幽處生雲烟」的境界以實物表達出來呢？

二十世紀現代文化兩大特徵：一是物質文明，科技先進；一是都市林立，生活緊張。什麼都是機械化、電腦化、標準化、公式化、大量生產化。人脫離了大自然。中國古典園林對自然材料的尊敬和應用，在科學發達的今天，更具啓發的特殊意義。

我希望透過這部「園林圖錄」，中國這個傳統的古老文化能夠得到普遍性、環球性的介紹；希望增加「人」對「自然因素」——一草一木、石、水、倒影的重新認識和愛好。更望從事設計的專家從中領悟其特徵和原理，在二十世紀的繁鬧都市穿插一些幽雅怡情的環境，使緊張的日常機械生活能有雲烟綠州的調和。

鍾華楠
一九八二年秋

園

歲在壬戌重夏恒夫書 楠園

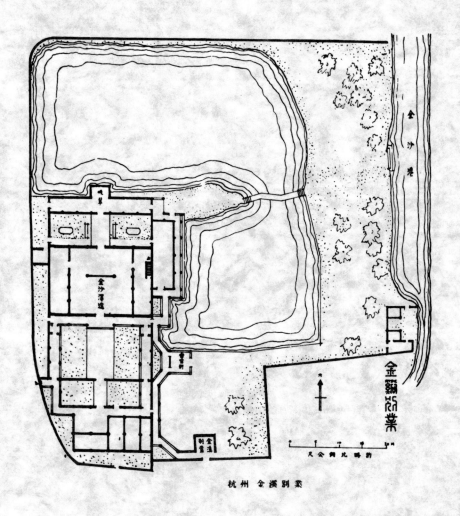

杭州 金溪金別業

「園」字是從中國園林之平
面圖的象形結構發展出來